Crazy in Love

Wild, Mushy, Hilarious Tales of Romance!

COSMO girl!
Crazy in Love

Wild, Mushy, Hilarious Tales of Romance!

From The Editors of CosmoGIRL!

Hearst Books
A Division of Sterling Publishing
Co., Inc.
New York

Book design by Margaret Rubiano

Published by Hearst Books
A Division of Sterling Publishing Co., Inc.
387 Park Ave. South, New York, NY 10016

CosmoGirl! is a trademark owned by Hearst Magazines
Property, Inc., in USA, and Hearst Communications,
Inc., in Canada. Hearst Books is a trademark owned by
Hearst Communications, Inc.

www.cosmogirl.com

For information about custom editions, special sales,
premium and corporate purchases, please contact
Sterling Special Sales Department at 800-805-5489
or specialsales@sterlingpub.com.

Distributed in Canada by Sterling Publishing
c/o Canadian Manda Group, 165 Dufferin Street
Toronto, Ontario, Canada M6K 3H6

Distributed in Australia by Capricorn Link (Australia)
Pty. Ltd. P.O. Box 704, Windsor, NSW 2756 Australia

Printed in China

ISBN 1-58816-490-X

From Me to You

Ah, love!!! Can't live with it, can't live without it, right? Yes, love can be frustrating, but it can also be great. That's why we're always on the quest for love. We're human, so we're kind of wired to be searching for that special someone to share our hopes, dreams, joys, sadness—and some smooches too, of course! But just because we all fantasize about love, that shouldn't mean that all you think about is getting a boyfriend. No way! I know from the letters and emails you send me that you've got tons more going on in your lives than just thinking about guys. Here's just a sampling of the other stuff you're doing: going shopping or to movies with your friends, writing poetry, perfecting your role in the school play, practicing your lay-ups with the rest of your basketball team, listening to your iPods, working out, babysitting, studying for SAT/ACTs or researching what colleges you might want to go to, throwing fundraisers for local charities, starting your own web-based graphic design companies, planning your prom—and yeah, at the end of the day, you might be thinking about your crush, or calling your main squeeze to tell him about the amazing (or crappy) day you just had. So the point is—love is one of your priorities, but not the be-all, end-all. You give it just the right amount of attention because it's fun to have love—real or fantasy—in your life...to hear your friends' stories and to tell them (and CG!) yours.

In this book, we've compiled tons of the BEST love stories you've ever told CG!—the craziest things you've done for someone, the wildest things guys have done for you, and the stupidest ways you've been dumped—and how you so smoothly overcame those bumps on the road of your love life. Have fun reading these and keep them coming to us at cosmogirl.com/lovestories. And I always want to hear from you at my personal email address at susan@cosmogirl.com. So keep dreaming about love—it's like ice cream—as long as you don't overindulge, it's good for your soul, CosmoGIRL!

Love,

Susan

StAte Of AfFaIrS

"My parents never let me date when I was in high school. Nonetheless, I had this adorable boyfriend who lived in another state (my parents didn't know about him), and for Christmas break and spring break I would go and visit him. How? I tricked my parents into letting me travel by saying it was for a 'class trip' or a 'ski club trip.' I always had them sign a parent-release form that I made up myself and printed out on my high school's letterhead!"

SaY ChEeSe

"This year for graduation, our entire class went on a trip to Hershey Park. My crush and I were both on this ride where your picture gets taken while you're on it. So I waited around until after my crush left, borrowed some money from one of my friends, and bought his pic for over $20! I still have it framed in my room, and not a day goes by that I don't look at it!"

healthy relationship

"My boyfriend and I had been dating for about a week and a half at the start of summer vacation. We saw each other every day and talked every night. But my mom wanted me to take health class in summer school so I could get it out of the way. My guy and I were sad that we wouldn't be able to spend as much time together. So the night before class started, he called to tell me that he had enrolled in health too, so that he could spend more time with me! And trust me, my boyfriend hates schools and lives for summer. We spent every day together that summer and we're still dating!"

BuTtAh BiNg!

"I wanted to ask this guy to the Sadie Hawkins dance, so I got a tub of butter and wrote a note on it that said, 'Dig to the bottom for your surprise.' I put it on his desk during first period but didn't put any surprise in there. Then, during second period, I put this bag of popcorn on his desk with a note that said, 'Sorry about first period, but I had to butter you up before I asked: Will you go to Sadie with me?' "

love BITES!

"For spring break I was on vacation with my family. I met this hot guy who was sleek and had a good tan. My sister told him that I like him and we started to talk. But, I didn't know he was bisexual. I was so into him, until one day he said, 'Look at that guy's butt. It is so tight.' I was shocked! I didn't know what to do, so I went home. We haven't talked since!"

GuY-JaCkInG

"I was at a school dance, and the last slow dance was about to play. I had been a chicken all night and hadn't asked my crush to dance, so I knew that this was my last opportunity—I could take it or leave it. I took it! But as I was walking over to him, I saw this other girl who liked him heading straight for him. She had already danced with him three times! So I ran up to her and told her I saw someone trying to steal her car out in the parking lot. She ran out of there so fast! Then I stole the last dance with my crush. She still thanks me, because she thinks I scared off a car thief!"

PaY DaTe

"One night, I was supposed to go on a date with my crush, but I got grounded and couldn't go. All night, my mom knocked on my door like every 10 minutes. I'd say, 'Still here,' and then she'd go away. I called my crush, Bryon, and told him what had happened, and he said he had an idea. Fifteen minutes later, there was a knock on my bedroom window (I'm on the ground floor). I looked out, and there was Bryon with his 14-year-old sister, Sydnee. She crawled in my window and told me to have a good time. I was like, *'What?'* Well, Bryon had paid Sydnee to say, 'Still here' so we could go out! I crawled out the window, hopped in Bryon's car, and had the night of my life. The next Monday, I saw Sydnee at school and asked her how much he paid her. She got $317 off him! Bryon and I are now dating, and I'm never going to let him go! And my mom never even found out what I did—I can't believe I never got caught."

PrIvAtE EyEs

"I was really obsessed with this guy named Michael. And since my best friend worked as an office aide at school, she could find out anything about almost anybody we wanted. So one day, she pulled up his personal file (she could have gotten expelled!) and got every detail about that boy—everything from his phone number to his birthday to his grades! And to this very day, he still doesn't know how I know so much about him! I always have to be really careful not to let too much information slip out whenever I'm talking to him."

tight spot

"My favorite Disney character is Tinker Bell, and I really wanted to dress up like her for Halloween. Just because he loves me so much, my boyfriend ended up dressing like Peter Pan to match me—green tights and everything! He actually went to school like that!"

PoLo MaTcH

"I met this great guy named Tim, and I really started to crush on him. We had talked sometimes but never really had anything more than that. Well, one day, at halftime during one of my water polo games, my coach told me that I was about to go in and play. But then I saw Tim up in the stands, and he was leaving! So I ran after him and said, 'Tim, I'm about to go in, you have to kiss me for good luck!' He was really shocked—but he kissed me. Talk about making a splash, right?"

FiTnEsS FrEaKs

"My best friend and I had crushes on these hot junior boys when we were freshmen in high school. We used to spend literally two to three hours at the gym after school every day so we could be in the same room as them and try to get their attention. (Trust me, we got to be in *great* shape!) We'd also just hang around until they'd give us rides home. Then when we were seniors in high school, the guys were back from college for break, and my friend and I finally hooked up with them. Mine was a great hook-up, but my best friend's sucked."

NiGhT Ow!-L

"My cutie and I had spent the whole day together, but when we talked at night, he said that he just had to see me again. Of course, I couldn't say no, but I was really nervous about sneaking out of the house. So I turned to my sister, the Queen of Sneak. She gave me elaborate instructions that entailed hanging on to the banister to avoid squeaky steps and climbing through the window of our storage room. I tried my best to follow her directions, but when it came to the storage room, I tripped over a pile of boxes and banged my toe on a filing cabinet. Then, when I tried to climb through the window, I got stuck in the frame! I managed to wriggle myself out and proceeded to fall five feet down, directly into a bush! Thank God my guy wasn't there to witness my elegant descent. After a lovely evening with him, I went back home—through the front door."

NiCe CaTcH

"I have lived next door to Josue since we were babies, but I didn't begin to like him until I turned 17. He never knew it, but I was *so* in love with him! One day, I bought tickets for both of us to go see a Cubs game in Chicago (he loves baseball). During the end of the ninth inning, I had arranged for a message to come up on the scoreboard. It said, 'Josue, I love you, and I've loved you for a long time.' When he read it, he looked at me in total surprise and said, 'Me too!' Then he hugged and kissed me. We've been together since."

DrAw HiM OuT

"I really wanted to go to the prom with this one guy, but I was too chicken to just go up and ask him. He was one of my really close friends, and we always sat by each other during classes we had together. Whenever we were in a class during a boring lecture or something, he'd let me draw on his arm with my gel pens, so one day during a lecture about history, I started to draw on his arm. I drew a few little hearts around one big heart and wrote, "Come to the prom with me." I turned away and looked back at the teacher, and then he wrote on my arm, "I thought you'd never ask. Of course I will." I still can't believe I actually *did* that!"

BaBy GoT BaCk

"Last summer, I went to the local pool frequently, not because I love to swim so much but because I was obsessed with this super-gorgeous lifeguard who worked there. On one occasion, the pool was doing free face painting for anybody who wanted it. I acted really brave and got the nerve to go up and get 'Aaron' drawn in a heart on my back. I then went and sat down in front of the lifeguard chair, exposing my back and letting him know how I felt. My act of bravery worked: Two days later, he asked for my phone number!"

stage presence

"One day in assembly, I saw my crush get up to make an announcement. He walked up onstage, looked at me, and said, 'Catherine, I wanted to know if you would go out with me. I have liked you for a long time!' I was so excited, I jumped up and screamed, 'Yes!' The bad part was that we both got detention. But we've been going out ever since!"

WeT 'n' WiLd

"My friend Michelle and I were walking along a beach in very cold weather when we saw some cute guys. My friend (who always needs attention) decided to push me in the lake for a laugh. When she gave me a shove, I grabbed her and pulled her in too! We got their attention all right, but not the way we would have liked—they all just stood there laughing while we almost drowned in our heavy, wet clothes!"

CaLL To ArMs

" I was at Six Flags on spring break and I wanted to find a hot guy to hang out with, so I bought a 'Free Hugs' hat and walked around with it on. Lots of guys gave me hugs, but only one was nice enough to actually start a conversation with me (after he had hugged me like 50 times). Now I'm so glad I bought that hat. I only wanted a guy for the day, but I got a boyfriend! We're still together!"

love BITES!

"I dated this guy who always made fun of things that weren't 'cool.' Well, I was in the senior play, Grease, and it was dorky—but so fun. On the day of the play, we all wore our costumes to school to advertise the show, but my boyfriend was so embarrassed I was wearing a poodle skirt that he ignored me all day. Then he started a fight so we'd break up—over a freakin' skirt!"

PiCkUP GaMe

"I had a crush on this cute dude for the longest time, but since we didn't have any classes together, I was pretty sure he didn't have a clue who I was. I wanted him to notice me, so whenever I saw him, I would drop something to get his attention—a book here, a pen there, my heart right in front of him! Finally, after about a month, I gave up. I figured he was a jerk since he never picked up one thing, and I had hinted really well that I liked him. Then one day when I thought my chances were blown, he walks right by me, looks me right in my eye, smiles at me, drops a note, and walks away. I'm no fool, so I picked up the note. It said, 'I like you. I thought I might pick up your habit.' Well, I nearly fainted right in the hallway! Since then, whenever we see each other, we drop little notes. Our relationship is still blossoming. Who knows what the next note will bring!"

BuRNInG DeSiRe

"My friends and I rented a beach condo for spring break in Panama City Beach, Florida. The place was nice and had a lot of space, so pretty much everyone we knew who was at the beach ended up staying there. One night the guy I had a crush on was over. The condo was crowded, so we went to the beach to be alone. I was exhausted, but we talked all night and I fell asleep right as the sun was coming up. Well, I have fair skin, and by the time the beach patrol woke me up, I was fried! My guy thought it was funny though, and we ended up going out for a couple of months after that!"

SwEeT SuCcEsS

"At my school, guys always ask girls to formals and dances in creative ways (like with puzzles and crosswords). So I decided to do something crazy like that for my crush so he would know I wanted him to ask me to a dance. I made him an extra-large cupcake that said 'Eat me' on top in icing. Between the layers, I placed a tiny card inside Saran Wrap that said 'I sit diagonally two seats behind you in English class. Ask me to the dance tomorrow. You know what my answer will be!' The window of his car was rolled down, so I put the cupcake on the front seat. Well, my plan worked, and he asked me to the dance! Later, he told me that he wasn't looking when he got into his car, and he sat on my cupcake! We've been dating for nine months, and he'll never let me forget about that!"

AmAzInG FiNiSh

"In gym class, we had a huge three-legged race, and we didn't get to pick our partners. Luckily, I ended up with the guy that I had a huge crush on—so we were tied together through the whole race! Well, at one point, we tripped, and he landed on top of me. I gave him this real flare look, and we started making out right in front of the whole class. Later that year, we were crowned prom king and queen."

class act

"It was my guy's and my four-month anniversary, and I wasn't going to be able to see him after school (I'm a cheerleader, and we had an away game that day). He knew I was really upset about it. I didn't know it at the time, but he skipped fourth period, our last period of the day, and got me four pink roses and a funny card. He came back to school, walked into the middle of my class while we were working and everything, and put them on my desk and left! Everyone in my class was clapping, and I was so happy, it made me cry!"

BoX TrOt

"I had the biggest crush on the most popular guy in school, and I wanted to tell him how I felt. So one day, all my friends and I went to his house to hang out. When he went to the bathroom, I opened one of his drawers and stole a pair of his blue-and-white boxers. To prove that I would do anything for him, the next day, I wore sweats with his boxers underneath, and I hung my pants down so he could see them! Big mistake! He and I are no longer friends. I guess he was just too weirded out!"

PoStCaRdS FrOm ThE EdGe

"There was this guy in my dorm who was so cute. I knew what his name was, but I'd never talked to him. Well, I was traveling a lot that semester, so for some reason, I thought it would be reasonable to send him postcards from every state I went to (like five in three months!) and just talk to him like we were old friends. I'd make up nicknames for him, compliment his new haircut...really ridiculous stuff. I never saw him again after that semester. I don't even think he knew who I *was!*"

It's a WrAp

"I'd only been dating this guy for about a week when Valentine's Day came up. I didn't know what to do for him since we hadn't been together that long. I decided to show him the true me and do something crazy—I figured he'd either be scared or just like me more. I got him candy and a card, and then I also decided to wrap myself up in a box and give *myself* to him for V-day. I got three of his friends to help me. They got a huge box, and I got inside. They wrapped up the box, and we decided to drive to his house with me on top of the car (he lives only six houses away from me). I was so scared! We got to his house only to realize he wasn't even home yet. He finally pulled up, and as he walked over to the car, his friends dropped the box (with me in it) onto the ground! The box broke, and I stumbled out onto his lawn! He said it was the cutest thing anyone had ever done for him. He and I are still together today and have *no* plans to break up."

LoVe NoTe

"I was in love with my best friend, Marco, but I was too nervous to tell him in person, so I decided to write him a note in my personal message in the yearbook (that the whole world would see!). I wrote, 'Marco, I'm in love with you. My dream is to marry you!' I was scared, but when we got our yearbooks, he told me that he felt the same way!"

SiNGInG TeLeGrAm

"Last year, I started dating this amazing guy, and we totally fell in love. But at the end of the year, an enemy started a rumor that I was interested in another guy (which was totally untrue!). I desperately tried to tell my boyfriend the truth, but he stopped answering his phone. Finally, the last day of school came, and a girl in our grade had a huge party. In order to get his attention, I went up onto the stage and announced to the entire party that it was all a lie by singing a love song my friends and I had just written! It was embarrassing—but he forgave me! Sometimes he asks for a repeat, but I tell him that was my one and only performance."

On ThE PrOwL

"I knew my crush had a crazy dog, because he'd always take him for walks by my house. So one day, I took home my friend's cat and let it out just as my crush walked by. The dog went crazy and started growling, then tore off chasing the cat—my crush and I had no choice but to follow! After an hour of searching for 'my expensive elderly cat,' we started talking. He asked me out the next day!"

road to recovery

"I'm from South Carolina and last summer I went to Florida on vacation. While I was there, I got in a car wreck and broke my arm. My boyfriend was so worried that he drove all the way to Florida on his motorcycle just to bring me flowers and make sure I was okay!"

BoOtY TrAp

"I went to camp at a college, and on the first night, I noticed this super-hot guy at dinner. My roommates and I saw him later as he was getting into the elevator, so I ran and stuck my hands in the elevator door so I could get in. Well, the doors got jammed after they opened about six inches, and everyone got stuck in there! It was my crush, two other guys, and a big, fat, old, mean guy who kept threatening to kill me when he got out. They were in there for an hour and a half! But hey, I got my crush's attention, which later led to a hook-up!"

PeE-YoU

"I was at the beach with friends, and I decided to go swimming. Bad idea! When I got in the water, I got stung by a jellyfish, and it hurt like hell. My crush said that pee is the only thing that takes the stinging pain away. Not thinking at all, I said to him, 'Well, then come *over* here and pee on my leg!' He was shocked—but he ended up peeing on my leg! We've been dating ever since!"

SnEaKY SaNtA

"In choir every year, we have a Secret Santa gift exchange. We give little presents every day for a week, and on the last day, we have a party where we reveal ourselves. Last year, my crush joined choir, and I was determined to be his Secret Santa. I didn't pick his name, but I found the guy who did and begged him to trade! Then, on the second-to-last day, I left him a fake invitation telling him that the party started an hour earlier than it really did. I talked to the people hosting the party, and I got there early to set up arrows that pointed upstairs. When my crush got to the party, he followed the arrows until he saw a sign that said, 'Close your eyes and come in.' He came in—and I kissed him! I said, 'Merry Christmas, Eric. I'm your last present.' He was stoked! It turns out *he* had traded with someone else to become *my* Secret Santa!"

YOU GLOW, GIRL!

"There was this guy I really liked at school. To get his attention, I bought a heart-shaped necklace that glows red when you turn it on. Every time I saw him in the hallway, which was often, I'd turn it on. After a week, he said, 'How does that thing *work*, anyway?' I said, 'It only works when I'm around you' and then walked away. That night, he called me and said, 'Well, if I had a necklace like that, it would glow red around you too,' and then he asked me out!"

ShAkEsPeArEaN ShOcKeR

"A new guy from Maryland started at our school. He was not only really hot but also a total sweetie, and I had the biggest crush on him. We became friends, but I wanted to be more than that. So one day in English class, we were all reading the play Romeo and Juliet. We picked the parts to read, and it just so happened that I was Juliet, and he was Romeo. We had to act out the balcony scene for the class, and at the end, when he said good night, I leaned in and kissed him!

The entire class started clapping, and my teacher just laughed. I guess my kiss impressed him: The next day, he asked me out!"

PiCkUp LiNe

"I really wanted to see my boyfriend, but his mom said I lived too far away and wouldn't drive him. So I told him to have her bring him to a gas station between us so that my mom and I could pick him up. What I really did was drive my mom's car there (I'm only 15!), parked, got into the passenger seat, and then pretended that my mom was in the store when they drove up!"

out of this world

"One night as I was leaving my boyfriend's house, he walked me to my car to give me a kiss good night. He kissed my forehead, and I looked up at the stars and saw this one really bright one. I said, 'Look at all the stars,' and I pointed to the bright one and said, 'That's our star.' But he wouldn't look—he just stared at me. So I told him to look again and he said, 'I am. I'm looking at my star.'"

PaY DaY

"I was dating this guy Blake, who my parents and my sister Lexxy totally hated. Well, I shared a room with Lexxy, but she always went to bed early! So I invited Blake over, and we stayed up all night cuddling and staring into each other's eyes. Eventually, we fell asleep. I woke up at 9 a.m., and my sister was standing over us with her mouth open. She promised not to tell anyone if I payed her $1 for every day we had been dating. I had to pay her $409! After that, she kept on saying, 'Krisi, why doesn't your boyfriend stay the night again? I won't tell!' "

GoOd-BYE GiRl

"I had been dating this girl I was crazy about, and she was spending her junior year abroad. I was really upset about it, so the day she was leaving, I called the airport to leave an "I'll miss you" message at the check-in desk. When she checked in, the clerk told her, 'Lindsey says she'll miss you a lot.' My girlfriend was so touched by it that she called me from one of the phones on the airplane!"

MeAt AnD GrEeT

"During our junior year, my friend and I both worked in the bakery at a grocery store. When this very sexy college freshman started working in the meat department, we instantly fell in love with him. We nicknamed him Mr. Beef, and we were basically obsessed with him. As the end of the school year approached, I knew I had to somehow get a pic of him before he left for the summer. So my friend and I made up this story about having a school project that involved where we worked. We took pictures of people in the other departments, but we mostly took pictures of the meat department. After telling Mr. Beef it was important to have him as part of our project, he agreed to have his picture taken. The catch was, we told him that I had to be in the picture with him, and we had to hold some of the meat! So he was holding a big bloody bone, and I had a package of pork chops. To this day, I still have the picture of us (with the meat!) in a frame on my desk."

BoY-AnCY ExPeRiMeNt

"One spring break I went on a cruise. On the first day I saw a cute boy, but I was scared to talk to him. Later that week, my friends and I went on a banana boat ride. I was nervous, but the cute guy was sitting right in front of me, so I couldn't back out. The boat started going really fast, and when we hit the first wave I went flying off! But when I opened my eyes, I realized that the cute guy had jumped into the water with me! He laughed as he helped me back onto the boat. We had fun together back on the cruise ship and we still talk on the phone."

HaNdY DaNdY

"It was my first day at an all-girls school I'd just transferred to, and I was feeling the place out. I had gym first period, and as I was sitting in the locker room, this hot girl came in. I couldn't help myself and kept looking over at her. I can't explain it, but we just had this connection. I didn't even ask if she was a lesbian—I just went over and grabbed her hand and gave it a soft kiss. At first, she looked at me funny—like she thought I was crazy—but then she started to smile. I can't believe that I found the girl of my dreams the first five minutes I was in a new school!"

SeT In StOnE

"I have liked the same guy for years. One day, his girlfriend made him kiss the ground after she walked over it. I thought it seemed as if he was being treated like a dog, but he enjoyed it (can you say *loser*?). Anyway, after everyone had gone inside, I grabbed some chalk and circled the area where he had kissed the ground. Then when school was over, I went home and got some tools, like a drill and all that stuff. After two hours, I finally got that piece of concrete out of the ground. To this day, I still have the piece of ground he kissed sitting on my dresser."

soldier of love

"My boyfriend of four months had to leave for the army, and I wasn't going to be able to see him for a whole year. The week that he was going to return, I received 11 red roses from him. I thought that was odd since 12 make up a dozen! Well, the day finally came for him to come home, and when he got off the plane, he held a red rose with something hanging off the end of it. I gave him a big hug, and right there in front of his whole family, he proposed to me! He told me that he just couldn't live without me ever again. Then he held me really tight and told me that he loved me!"

SiGnS Of LoVe

"I had a major crush on this guy who swam at the pool I worked at. He was really hot—and available. Only one problem: He was deaf. So I went to the library and checked out 15 books on learning sign language. I learned the basics, and the next time I saw him, I said hi in sign language. We became friends, and now we've been going out for nearly three months!"

StAgE HaNd

"I was madly in love with a guy named Craig, so I wrote him a love song. We were in a play together, and at the end of opening night, I brought him out onstage and sang my song to him. I felt faint, wondering what his reaction would be. The crowd clapped for me even though they didn't really understand what was going on. Craig was stunned, but he leaned in and kissed me. We've been together ever since!"

DrIvE-iN DaTe

"My friends and I were cruising around town, and I saw this really hot guy next to us at a stoplight. So before the light turned green, I pulled out in front of his car so he couldn't go anywhere, then I got out and asked him if he would go on a date with me! Amazingly, he said yes! So I gave him my number, and now, two years later, we're engaged!"

GeT WeLl CaRt

"Last winter, I slipped on the stairs to my apartment and really hurt my knee. I had problems walking and had to have it bandaged up for the longest time. One Saturday, I was really looking forward to seeing my boyfriend, only that morning, he called to say that he couldn't pick me up because he caught the flu. I don't have a car, and his house is about a 45-minute walk away from my place. I was still having problems with my knee, but I *really* wanted to see him, so I made some soup and put it in a Thermos and bundled myself up. There's this elderly man with a wheely cart I always see around town. While I was walking, I ran into him, and he was on his way to get groceries, so he had this really large basket attached to the back of his wheely cart. He knew I was having knee trouble, so he let me sit in the basket and 'drove' me the whole way! My boyfriend was laughing so hard when I 'pulled up!'"

HeAd OvEr HeEls

"One time, my boyfriend dared me to sneak out of my house in the middle of the night while my parents were sleeping and meet him at a park. I took the dare. While I was climbing out my bedroom window, I fell and hit the dirt—face first. When I got to the park, I had blood all over my face and T-shirt. He just looked at me and said, 'You don't just like me—you love me!'"

love BITES!

"I was going out with the hottest, nicest guy ever—or so I thought. One day we went to the movies and I put my head on his shoulder. After that, for six days he acted really weird; then he dumped me! I found out from his friend that he said I was annoying at the movies! I mean, *loser*!"

better than hot wings

"The night of our five-month anniversary, my boyfriend picked me up to go to dinner at Chili's. On our way there he told me he had left his wallet at home. We were driving to his house when he turned down a dirt road. I thought it was strange, but he said he had a surprise for me. At the end of the road was a table decorated with a lace tablecloth, roses, citronella candles (to keep the bugs away), glasses for tea, lasagna, and bread. Then he gave me a promise ring because he was leaving for college! It was so romantic!"

PaInT By NuMbErS

"Me and my boyfriend had been together for three and a half years when we had the biggest argument ever. We didn't talk for two weeks, and when we finally did, we agreed to be just friends. But I still loved him with all my heart, so I decided to get his attention. We had a code for 'I love you'—'143.' So I took posters and painted '143' on them and put them on all the stop signs and telephone poles around my house because that was the route he took to his mom's. They were *everywhere*. When he saw them that day, he called me on his cell phone and said, '143 too!' Now we're back together, and things are going great!"

BuBbLeGuM HoP

"Me and my boyfriend were at a school dance when we kissed the first time (it was also the first time he told me he loved me). He was chewing gum when he kissed me, and he slipped it into my mouth! Well, I wanted to keep a memento of the night, so I saved the ticket stub from the dance. But I saved something else too: I chewed that piece of gum *all* night so I could take it home and keep it. Three years later, I still have that piece of chewed-up gum in a Ziploc bag in my dresser drawer!"

CoMiNg OuT EaSt

"A few years after I graduated from high school and had come out, I realized I had a crush on a girl I used to row with my junior year. I was living on the west coast and had to drive out east for college. I hadn't seen this girl since graduation, and she had no idea I was interested in women, but I called her up and asked her to drive cross country with me! She said she couldn't make the trip at that time but she'd take a bus out to see me later. About three weeks later, she arrived.

We had only planned on spending a few days together, but we ended up dating. Turns out she had a crush on me too but didn't know I was into women!"

SoLe MaTeS

"I had a major crush on this guy in my class, so I decided to make a plan. One day, when he was standing at his locker, I 'accidentally' dropped my folder on my shoe right in front of him. Well, he was nice enough to bend down to pick up my folder for me. He said, 'Is this yours?' And as he lifted the folder off my shoe, suddenly he smiled...I'd written 'Can you go out with me to a movie?' on it— and he said yes! We've now been dating for a year."

Ab-SaLuTe DeVoTiOn

"I sing lead in a band. This one time, my band was asked to play at a surprise party. The person the party was for was a good friend of the band—and the guy I was secretly in love with. I figured this was my last chance to tell him how I felt since he was turn-ing 18 and joining the army, so I asked my bandmates if we could open with a slow, sexy 'Happy Birthday.' They agreed, and I decided to make a big show out of it by putting together a special outfit. I wore my cousin's marineuniform jacket and hat, and my camouflage skirt (a sort of salute to him!). When he walked into the party, I was in this military getup, in front of all our friends, singing 'Happy Birthday' right to his face. I basically made a fool of myself, but he loved it!"

KeEp TrUcKiN'

"I was dating this guy who was way into trucks. He always said he loved girls who drove them, so when I finally got my own ride, I asked for a black Chevy pickup. The relationship ended up fizzling a few weeks later, and now I'm stuck with a huge Z71 and no guy! Did I mention it sucks climbing into the cab in heels?"

gut feeling

"One day I left school early because I had bad cramps. I called my boyfriend and he ditched his class to come see me. We hung out for a little while, but when he was about to leave, instead of giving me a good-bye kiss on the lips, like he usually does, he kissed my tummy to make it feel better! If you don't think that's cute and loving, then I don't know what is!"

BoX TrOt

"I had the biggest crush on the most popular guy in school, and I wanted to tell him how I felt. So one day, all my friends and I went to his house to hang out. When he went to the bathroom, I opened one of his drawers and stole a pair of his blue-and-white boxers. To prove that I would do anything for him, the next day, I wore sweats with his boxers underneath, and I hung my pants down so he could see them! Big mistake! He and I are no longer friends. I guess he was just too weirded out!"

SuGaR BaBe

"I'd had a crush on this guy for almost six months, and I was sick of waiting for him to ask me out, so I decided to take matters into my own hands. I made a treasure hunt, starting with a note in his locker. It led him all over the school and eventually back to his house, where I was waiting with a big plate of cookies and a sign that said WILL YOU BE MY SUGAR RUSH? I know it's cheesy, but it worked! We've been going out for two years!"

SwEeT SuCcEsS

"At my school, guys always ask girls to formals and dances in creative ways (like with puzzles and crosswords). So I decided to do something crazy like that for my crush so he would know I wanted him to ask me to a dance. I made him an extra-large cupcake that said 'Eat me' on top in icing. Between the layers, I placed a tiny card inside Saran Wrap that said 'I sit diagonally two seats behind you in English class. Ask me to the dance tomorrow. You know what my answer will be!' The window of his car was rolled down, so I put the cupcake on the front seat. Well, my plan worked, and he asked me to the dance! Later, he told me that he wasn't looking when he got into his car, and he sat on my cupcake! We've been dating for nine months, and he'll never let me forget about that!"

DaRiNg TrUtH

"I had this guy friend who I never thought was cute—but I never thought he was ugly either. As we got to be better friends, I fell in love! One day, we were hanging out and started playing truth or dare. When I picked truth, he asked me what I'd do if I could do anything in the world. My response? I kissed him! And I guess my friend liked it because we started dating and have been together ever since!"

WrItE On

"I just couldn't get this cute guy Derek off my mind. So when it finally came time to sign our yearbooks, I went up and asked to write in his. At the end of the note, I wrote, 'Why don't you ask me out this summer?' and then gave it back to him. Later that day, Derek came up to me and said, 'Why should I wait until this summer—want to go out with me on Friday?' I was so incredibly shocked I almost forgot to say yes!"

love BITES!

"I'd been dating this guy for a month and things were going well. I thought we'd be together for a long time and that he was mature. Then one day his friend came up to me and said, 'Well, I have good news and bad news. The bad news is that your boyfriend doesn't want to go out with you anymore. The good news is that I just saved a ton of money on my car insurance by switching to Geico!' I was about to cry, but what he said was so funny, I just fell over laughing."

McHoTtIe

"Everyone said that my crush liked me, but he never asked me out. Then his friends told me he was working part-time at McDonald's so he could get a nicer car before he asked me out. Instead of waiting, I went to his work, walked right up to his cash register, and said, 'Hi, I need a large fry, a medium coke, and a boyfriend.' He just jumped right over the counter and kissed me!"

fantasy island

"My family was planning a huge trip to Hawaii for spring break last year, and I had been looking forward to it for months and months. But a week before spring break, my grandma had a stroke. My family had to fly to Nowhereville, Kansas, and our Hawaii trip was canceled because my grandma died. My boyfriend knew how upset I was—I was very close with my grandma, and I had really been looking forward to the trip to Hawaii. One night, we had plans to go see a movie, and we were meeting at his house. When I got there, he put a Hawaiian necklace around my neck and attached one of those grass skirts around my waist, and we danced. He had decorated his whole living room with pictures and wall hangings of Hawaii, and hula music was playing on his stereo. We sat under a paper palm tree, and he whispered to me that he hoped it was almost as good as going to Hawaii. It definitely was!"

OuT Of TuNe

"I was madly in love with this guy, but he didn't feel the same way about me. Still, when we went to separate colleges, I called him occasionally, and I even wrote a song about him. I made copies of the song and started handing out tapes on campus. Well, he must have found out because I was slapped with a restraining order and am now in danger of a $500 fine for stalking!"

SaCk AtTaCk

"It was my first Valentine's Day with a boyfriend, so I wanted to make it extra special. Inspired by a potato sack I'd found at a garage sale, I decided to 'kidnap' my boyfriend after class with the help of my older brother and his friend. I got permission from my teacher to leave class 10 minutes early so I could set up. My brother backed up his truck so the bed was right at the bottom of the stairs at one of the school exits. As my boyfriend walked out of class, I screamed, 'Surprise!' and snapped a picture before my brother and his friend threw the sack over his head, hog-tied him, and tossed him into the truck. We drove to the beach, where I'd set out a blanket covered with rose petals and a cooler full of his favorite foods. Let me just say, the pictures were priceless!"

pick of the litter

"My boyfriend of two years knows that I absolutely love animals, especially cats. I have a cat of my own, but because I spend most of my time at my boyfriend's house, I always miss my kitty. One day, when I thought my guy was off tutoring, he walked into my room with a huge cardboard box that had 'Open Me' written on it. Inside was a 6-week-old calico he had gotten for himself! We had to hide it from his parents for a week, but finally he persuaded them to 'get a kitten.' I was amazed that he did something so out of character to make me happy!"

BaLlS-Y MoVe

"I had a huge crush on this guy on the basketball team. I would see him all the time because I was on the dance line, and we always practiced in the gym while the basketball team was running their drills. One day, I snuck into the gym before practice and wrote 'I love Josh' in permanent ink all over their practice basketballs. When the team came out to the gym, the coach started going crazy and yelling at everyone. I ended up having to buy 20 new basketballs— but I did *get* my guy!"

DrIvInG MiSs SpAcEy

"This gorgeous guy and I had been driving alongside each other for a while, making eye contact, smiling, flirting...you know, the whole bit. I noticed he was going to make a left turn, and I wanted to keep flirting with him, so I quickly switched lanes and followed. We turned onto a small residential street and started talking through our windows, driving about five miles an hour. I didn't quite know where I was, and I wasn't really watching the road either. That must have been why this fire hydrant suddenly jumped out at me!

I slammed on my brakes—but not before the front end of my car was totally dented, and the hottie was laughing hysterically. He ended up asking for my number, but it cost me nearly $200 to fix the car, plus I got a ticket for the hydrant. Was it really worth it? Yeah!"

BoArDeR LiNe

"My first anniversary with my boyfriend was coming up, and I wanted to get him the absolute perfect gift for this very special occasion. His favorite thing in the world is snowboarding, but his board was in pretty bad shape. So I got one of his close friends to casually ask around and find out the exact kind of board he wanted. Then I went out and bought him this expensive new board with the money I was saving up to get a new computer. I even sprung for a really cool carrying case for it. He loved it so much, he brought his board to work with him the next day. It was definitely worth the three months of paychecks that I'd been saving!"

class act

"It was my guy's and my four-month anniversary, and I wasn't going to be able to see him after school (I'm a cheerleader, and we had an away game that day). He knew I was really upset about it. I didn't know it at the time, but he skipped fourth period, our last period of the day, and got me four pink roses and a funny card. He came back to school, walked into the middle of my class while we were working and everything, and put them on my desk and left! Everyone in my class was clapping, and I was so happy, it made me cry!"

LaYiNg ClAiM

"I liked this guy, and when my friend started to like him too, I just *had* to claim him. So I volunteered to announce the school talent show at assembly. But after my announcement, I added some things—like the fact that I was in love with him. He didn't say anything at first, but he called me later that night and asked me to go out!"

Dr. FeElGoOd

"My boyfriend found out a few months ago that he has cancer, and he's now going through chemotherapy. He has this beautiful, long hair that I love, but he's starting to go bald in places from the treatments. He was always so sure of himself before, but now he's worried about how he looks. So to help make him feel okay with everything, I cut my own hair super-short and bought these really cute matching bandannas for us to wear on our heads all the time. The style is not really 'me,' but he is feeling so much better since I got us the new look!"

NuT So GoOd

"I'm really allergic to nuts, but the first time I ever went over to my boyfriend's house, he started trying to be all cute by feeding me this fruit-and-nut bar. I didn't want to say anything to embarrass him, so I just decided to eat it anyway, hoping I'd be okay. I ended up having such a bad reaction that we had to call an ambulance to come and rush me to the hospital!"

MaLe DeLiVeRY

"I live in Utah, but every summer, I have to fly to Washington, DC, to spend a month with my dad. I had only been with my boyfriend for about five weeks when I had to leave last summer, and we were both really bummed that I had to go. So I made this huge package for him with one envelope for each day I'd be gone, and then filled them with little surprises and letters. On the ninth day, my boyfriend opened up his envelope—and found a plane ticket. He flew out, and we got to watch the 4th of July fireworks together! Now *that's* a tradition I hope to keep!"

DiGiTaLlY MaStErEd

"My boyfriend was really depressed because he was at one college and I was at another really far away. We had never been apart like that, so he was sad that we didn't get to see each other every day like normal. He was always telling me that he missed just being able to know what I was doing, even if it was boring day-to-day stuff. So I got a great idea. I borrowed my roommate's digital camera and started taking pictures of myself doing all the silly little rituals that I do each day—brushing my teeth in the dorm bathroom, eating lunch outside on the quad, studying in the library.... Then, in each picture, I wore a homemade sign around my neck that said 'Missing you now.' That way, he knew that I was thinking about him all the time, even though he wasn't there with me. He loved it so much that we started doing that once a month, always trying to outdo each other. Now we *always* feel like we're together, even when we have to be apart."

FLAg HiM DoWn

"I was at a club with my friends, and there was this *gorgeous* DJ! I wanted him to notice me, so when he asked for a volunteer for stand-up karaoke, I thought it was my chance! I screamed and hollered, and he chose me! But what *wasn't* so good was that I had to pick my own song, and the only one I could think of was 'You're a Grand Old Flag.' *But* the DJ told me later on that I had a beautiful voice, and he asked for my number! *Score!*"

street smart

"There was this guy I was, like, in love with, and we had started to talk. I found out that he lived near me, so one day, I had my friend walk up to his house with me. He wasn't home, but the next day, my friend told him that we had walked up there. After he found that out, he supposedly started coming to my house a lot, but he said that I was never there when he showed up. I told him to write his name on my sidewalk the next time he came over to prove he was there. Sure enough, the next day, his name was on my sidewalk in pink chalk.

We started leaving each other little notes in chalk on each other's sidewalks. After about a week, he asked me out (with chalk on my sidewalk), and we've been going out ever since!"

SwEeT 17

"I was totally obsessed with this guy—I asked him out practically every day for an entire year! But he always said no. One day, my parents told me that we were moving, and I was devastated. I had to do something to get him before I left—so I *paid* him 17 bucks to kiss me! Now, whenever I talk with friends about first kisses, I get to say, 'I paid someone for my first kiss.' "

OpEn-DoOr PoLiCy

"I was obsessed with this guy I'd never talked to but always saw. I wondered what he was like. So one day, I noticed his locker was slightly open. I figured it wouldn't hurt if I just peeked, you know, to see if I could find out *something*. Well, I got so absorbed in everything, I didn't notice that he had walked up behind me! At first, I was panicked, but then I realized this was my big chance. I said, 'Um, you left your locker open, and you always looked so interesting, I wanted to find out about you. I hope you don't mind.'

He kind of stood there thinking for a second, then said, 'Actually, that's the coolest thing anyone's ever said to me.' We ended up sitting in the deserted hall and talking for over two hours!"

RoAd WaRrIoR

"My boyfriend and I got into this huge fight, and he told me he wasn't arguing anymore and then left. I was a nervous wreck and didn't know what to do, so I got in my mom's Camry and took off while my dad was in the house. (I'm only 15, and in the state of Kentucky, you don't even get your permit until you're 16.) I ended up following my boyfriend five miles until he stopped! My parents never found out!"

ScReEn TeAm

"After a date with my crush, I used my friend's screen name (with permission) to talk to him. Since they were good friends, I pretended to be her and asked him, 'Hey, did you have a fun time today?' He told me just about everything he thought of me, not knowing he was telling *me*! I even gave him pointers on what he should do to go out with me. He never found out because I told my friend what we had talked about, so she was able to carry on the conversation at school. It totally worked! We started going out!"

ThE PeRfEcT PlAn

"On the first day of school, there was a total cutie sitting right next to me. After talking to him, I just knew I had to ask him out. I found out that his birthday was soon, so I came up with a plan. The morning of his birthday, I woke up really early. I bought two orange balloons and one yellow (his favorite colors). I also tied a Snickers bar (his favorite candy bar) to the bottom of them. I taped them to his locker with a note that said, 'Happy Birthday! Dinner Friday? My treat, of course. You tell me where.' To make a long story short, he said yes, and we went out that Friday!"

❤ love BITES!

"I had a major crush on this senior named Venson. I was totally obsessed, even though I wasn't sure he even knew I existed! So, for his birthday, I bought him a silver bracelet with his name engraved in it. I didn't tell him who had sent it to him. A couple of days later, I asked my friend to go up and ask Venson what he thought of the bracelet. She did and he said that he pawned it to buy parts for his car. That was all it took to kill *that* obsession!"

In THE FlEsH

"This guy and I had been dating for out entire sophomore year of college, and I really wanted to show him that I was totally in love with him. So for our one-year anniversary, I got this tattoo of his name on the small of my back. It was really cute, and I thought that he would really love it. But I was wrong—it completely freaked him out, and he broke up with me. Now I am stuck with this jerk's name tattooed on my back, and I just found out that it costs like five times more to have it removed than it actually cost to get the thing!"

grassroots effort

"I was dating this guy who said he had a surprise present for me. Well, the next morning, I woke up to my mom yelling. When I walked downstairs to see what she was so upset about, I discovered that my boyfriend had spray-painted 'I LOVE YOU' in huge red letters out front! My parents are completely obsessive about the yard, so they totally freaked out. Worst of all, it had to stay there until the grass was long enough to be cut again!"

MoOnLiGhT MiLeS

"I have been in a long-distance relationship for almost two years now—I go to school, and he works far away from me. We normally only get to see each other once every two months, but one weekend, I decided that as a surprise, I'd make a spontaneous trip up to see him. I planned everything out perfectly: I skipped a whole day of classes so I could do the eight-plus-hour drive, and I told my boyfriend I'd be out with a friend so he wouldn't try to call me on my cell phone. When I pulled up in front of his house that night, I called him and said that the moon was so beautiful that he should go outside and look. When he opened the door, I was standing there on the front stoop. He nearly fell over backward from the shock!"

SaNd-ScRiPt

"I was at my family's beach house and decided to go for a walk. When I walked out of the house, there was this amazingly hot guy standing alone at the water. We kind of looked at each other, but I kept walking. When I got back, I noticed he was still in front of the house. I'm not really sure what gave me the courage, but I walked right up to him, wrote my cell number in the sand, and walked away. The next day at the beach, he came up to me and wrote his digits in the sand too! We've been talking to each other on the phone ever since!"

MaTcH PoInT

"Last summer, I met this amazingly hot guy near my beach house. There was one problem: He was my tennis instructor at my country club! At the end of the summer, there was this big tournament for the best female tennis player. I was okay at tennis—but not good enough to win. So to impress him, I went to the courts by myself for about two hours after lessons each day to practice. I didn't win the tournament, but I did end up getting second! And the instructor pulled me aside afterward and told me that he saw me practicing a couple of times while he was closing the guys' locker rooms. I felt really stupid, but luckily, he thought it was cool that I had worked so hard—and we went out a lot during the rest of my summer vacation. I guess hard work really does pay off!"

SiGnAtUrE MoVe

"There was a gorgeous girl named Jill who I had my heart set on all summer. I knew she loved Blink-182, so when I went to their concert that summer, I hung around the backstage door until the band finally came out, and I made them sign a T-shirt. Then on the first day of school, I waited to see her in the hall and handed her the shirt. She gave me a surprised look and asked me why I'd gone through all the trouble. I told her about my massive crush on her. She asked me out to lunch for the next day and confessed that she had a crush on *me*! We've been dating for two years now!"

lovesick

"Okay, I wasn't feeling well one weekend, and I had a big project due on Monday. Since I spent all Saturday sick and all Sunday working on my project, I couldn't see my boyfriend that weekend, which meant I would have to wait until the next weekend because we live in different towns. Well, around 6 p.m. on Sunday, he called me and said, 'Look outside—you might be able to see me.' He had ridden his bike six miles to my house in the freezing cold to give me a teddy bear because I was sick!!!"

GeT RiCh QuIcK

"I had a huge crush on this guy Rich who lived three doors down the street from me. I mean, he was seriously the most perfect guy I could ever imagine! I knew he was really into working out and running, so during my freshman year in high school, I decided to join the cross-country running team. I never would've done that if it wasn't something I knew he was totally into, but it turned out that I had an *awesome* year. I ended up being one of the best girls on the team, which completely gave my crush and me something to talk about. Now we talk to each other every day at practice—definitely worth it!"

WhItE HoT

"It was my first year in high school, and I was crushing on this junior who I met on the swim team. I overheard him tell his friend about how he loved girls who wore white bikinis. So the next week, instead of coming to swim team in my practice suit, I showed up in a brand-new white two-piece. Not only did my coach almost kick me off the team for being out of uniform, but the guy thought I was a total wacko! So much for *that* relationship."

FoReIGN AfFaIr

"My boyfriend was studying abroad and we were both really sad that we weren't going to be able to see each other in person on the night of our three-year anniversary. I was interning at my uncle's law firm at the time, and the office had this really cool video-conferencing system, meaning you can see and hear the other person in real time. So I got this idea: I begged my uncle for like two weeks to let me use it until he finally caved, then I mailed my boyfriend a Web camera and pretended that it was his anniversary present. On the actual night of our anniversary though, I called my boyfriend and told him to go check his e-mail, where I'd sent him this hyperlink. When he finally opened up the link, it was me sitting there talking to him! Once he got his Web cam up and working, we were able to have a face-to-face date for our anniversary!"

ShAdOw BoXeR

"I was so in love with this boy that I saved everything in a box that reminded me of him, even clippings from newspapers *just* because they said his name (even if the articles weren't really about him!). I'd even follow him, and whenever he'd throw something away, I'd wait until he was gone— then go dig it out of the trash and keep it in the box! By the end of the year, the box was full, but he still didn't know my name!"

DeTeNtIoN GeTtEr

"I have been in love with this total 'bad boy' since fall semester, when we had classes together. But at my high school, our schedules change every semester, and we didn't have any of the same classes that spring. So I tried to think of some way to see him....Well, he was always getting into trouble at school, and I knew he had detention almost once a week, so I started intentionally being late for school a lot (if you're late three times, you get detention). We talked and flirted in detention, and I kept figuring out these little ways to get back into detention. But little did I know after four detentions, you get Saturday school. I ended up not only having Saturday school but also having a parent-teacher conference about my behavior! In the end, the guy thought it was totally cool that I sacrificed my reputation to talk to him. We stayed together for over a year!"

BoTtOmS UP

"My crush and I were going on a group trip to visit college campuses. I knew he loved girls with a sense of humor, so out of the blue, I decided to moon the people in the cars behind us from the back of the van. One of them was this lady who followed us to the next rest stop. She told my adviser what I'd done, and I ended up getting two weeks of detention! But my crush laughed so hard, he *cried*. We've been dating ever since!"

back in action

"I was moving out of my sorority house into an apartment, so I asked this guy I had just started dating if he could help me move. I didn't think it would be a big deal because my bed, desk, and dresser belonged to the sorority house and were staying there. Well he came over, and we'd started loading things into my car when I offered to run and get lunch for us. I ended up getting stuck in a long line for 30 minutes. When I got back, he had lugged all of the big furniture that wasn't supposed to leave my room out to the sidewalk—and it was so heavy that he pulled his back moving it!"

OsCaR PeRfOrMaNcE

"My boyfriend and I were in the same speech class when he decided that we needed to 'take time off.' I was totally upset because the reason he wanted to do this was that he thought I was cheating on him with my best guy friend—but I totally wasn't. Well, one of our assignments in the class was to write a persuasive speech. So I decided to give a speech on why he should *not* break up with me. I was a little embarrassed that I did it in front of the whole class, but he was really impressed with what I said. We got back together after my speech—and I also got an A because I presented it with such strong points!"

PlEdGe Of LoVe

"I had a huge crush on this guy in my biology class. He was the hottest kid in my high school, and I wanted him to take me to my prom. Well, I'm school president, and every day I do our announcements over the intercom. Right in the middle of the Pledge of Allegiance I said, 'one nation, under Brent taking Sara to the prom, indivisible....'" He loved it so much, we even ended up going to the same college, where we're still dating!"

HoLe In OnE

"The guy I had a crush on was working as a caddy at the golf course, so I begged the manager for a job driving the beverage cart around. There is this sign on the front of the cart that says the price of all the drinks and stuff, so I decided I'd switch the sign with this huge, homemade one saying 'Honk if you think David should ask me out!' Later that day, I saw him on the second to last hole of the course and knew that if I didn't just drive by right then with my sign, I'd never do it.

I got up the nerve, drove really slowly by him, and started honking. All of the men that he was caddying for started laughing, but they ended up giving him this awesome tip and telling him to take me out to dinner that night. So he did—and we had the most amazing time ever!"

ExTrA CrEdIt

"Freshman year of college, a friend found out that my crush was in a big biology lecture on Tuesdays that had over 150 people in the class. I figured no one would notice if I sat in on the class a few times—but I had so much fun doing it, I ended up pretending to be in his class the entire semester. They didn't take attendance, and tests were given in groups on different days, so no one ever knew I wasn't part of the class. I got to go on study dates with my crush all semester long!"

SlEePiNg BeAuTy

"I was going on a road trip to a theme park with some friends, and I was so excited because my crush was going to be riding in the same car as me. We decided to drive through the night and take turns sleeping so we could get there the next morning before the lines got long. I drove the first shift, and my crush was supposed to drive after me. Well, I looked over, and he was asleep—but he looked so sweet, I just couldn't wake him up. I drove on but started to get so sleepy, I couldn't keep my eyes open. I thought that maybe if I pulled over, I could take a short nap and be okay. Well, the next thing I knew, my crush was shaking me awake—it was morning! Everyone, including my crush, was mad at me for the rest of the trip—especially when they saw the mile-long lines once we finally got to the park!"

FeEt Of CoUrAgE

"My family was on a vacation at Disney World. One day, in line for a ride, there was this total cutie who I was too shy to talk to. He was gorgeous—tan skin, brown hair, blue eyes, and a *great* bod. I wanted to get his attention, so I paid my little brother $50 to run up and step on his foot. Then I had an excuse to go up to him—I started apologizing for my little brother's awful behavior. We laughed about it and then hung out together for the rest of my vacation!"

dirty dozen

"I was in history class when there was a knock on the door. The teacher opened it, and there stood my boyfriend holding a rose! She let him come in to give it to me, but the entire class was laughing at us. It wasn't so bad—except that he did the same thing in every class that day! By the end of the day, he'd given me a dozen roses—and everyone knew it!"

SwEeT EmOtIoN

"I really liked this guy and I wanted to ask him to our Sadie Hawkins dance, but I wanted to do it in an unusual way. So I went and made my own plate at a ceramics store that said 'Will you go to Sadie's with me?' with a poem right under it. Then I baked cookies and put them on top of the plate. I left them on his weight-lifting bench in the gym because I knew he worked out right after school. The next day, he came up to me, gave me a hug, and said, 'Thanks for the cookies, and yes, I'll go with you!' I can't believe it worked!"

love **BITES!**

"I was dating this guy, and things were going great—until Valentine's Day rolled around. The week before, the dude suddenly breaks up with me with some bogus explanation that he wasn't 'feeling it right now.' Well, later on, I found out from his friend that the _real_ reason he broke up with me was so he wouldn't have to spend money on a Valentine's Day present! What a _loser!_"

CrAsH CoUrSe

"I was about to get my license— but not for another couple of weeks. Well, at the mall, I met this total hottie who was a few years older than me, so I lied and said I was his age and that I went to a different school in the area. He invited me to a party and then asked me if I could pick him up. I would have said no, but my parents were going away for the weekend, and I thought, What the heck? I took my mom's car and drove over to his house, but when I was pulling into his driveway, I ran right into his mailbox! When my parents got home, they saw the dent in the car and were furious. Not only was I immediately grounded until further notice, I haven't spoken to the guy since!"

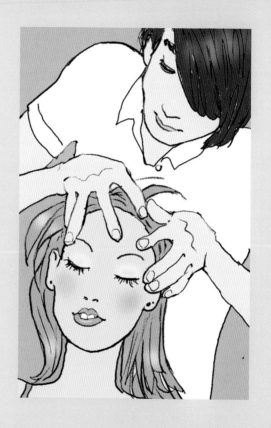

Ex-TrA EfFoRt

"I was spending the night at my friend's house and kept telling her how much I missed my ex, who broke up with me over some rumors that weren't true. I guess she got tired of hearing me blab about him, so at four in the morning, she insisted on driving me to his house so I could tell him how I felt. When we got there, I really wanted to go back, but it was too late. So I went up to the door and knocked, and to my surprise, he was up and opened it! He looked shocked because I hadn't been there since we'd been split up. It turns out that he missed me too—but was scared to say anything! We've been happily together ever since!"

ExTrA ScOoP

"I work as a student reporter for my city newspaper, and this one time, they wanted me to interview some guy from our city who was selected to go to this amazing leadership conference in Washington, DC. Turns out, this mystery guy was a hottie who'd recently graduated from my high school. When we shook hands at the interview, I knew something clicked between us—plus, he had adorable dimples that completely mesmerized me! But he was leaving to go to the conference in DC the next day and wouldn't be back in town for another three weeks. So I got his number in case I needed to ask any follow-up questions, then called him in DC for 'updates.' After a couple of all-night talks, he came back home as my new boyfriend!"

SwEeT SpOt

"It was my boyfriend's birthday, and he was dying for a specific kind of chocolate cake. But it was a bit tricky because one, the bakery that made it was four hours away, and two, I didn't have a car. So I had to take the bus all the way there. And on the return trip, I had to buy the cake its own freakin' seat!"

boarder line

"My ex was so crazy. On Valentine's Day last year, he actually skateboarded six miles to give me roses and chocolates. Thing is, he could have just waited and given them to me at school! That's eventually why we broke up—the poor guy was just too dedicated!"

GaMe Of LoVe

"My boyfriend and I have been together since last year, and I wanted to do something totally original for his birthday. We love to go paintballing together, so I decided to buy him a box of 500 paintballs and write 'I love you' on every single one of them. It took me almost three days to finish the job, but we had such a blast putting them to use—and now he's more in love with me than ever!"

DrIvE Me CrAzY

"I had a crush on this girl who worked at the school paper with me in Maryland. Over winter break, she needed to go to the office to work on a story. Since I am one of the top editors at the paper, I had a key to the office, but she didn't. So I volunteered to let her in—even though I was three and a half hours away in Pennsylvania! I drove all the way there and waited in the office as she worked. She told me it was okay if I left, but I stayed. When she was done, I had to drive all the way back home to go to work that night—but I didn't tell her. A few weeks later, we started dating, and when I told her about the scheme, she just laughed at me."

RoCkY's RoAd

"My two-year pursuit of my friend, Rocky, was bordering on obsession. I was so into him that whenever I drove around the city, I kept my eyes peeled for his striped truck, just in case it might give me a secret glimpse of him. One night, a bunch of us were going to meet up for a movie, but Rocky never showed. Turns out, his truck was stolen! I knew how much Rocky loved his truck, so, relying on my semistalker habits, I searched the street for those familiar stripes. Within a few days, I actually found the truck parked on some random street corner! I told Rocky, and we went to recover it together. Of course, this didn't magically make him fall in love with me (even though his mom referred to me as his 'angel'). But we are still friends today, and Rocky is still really grateful that I found his truck."

CuT To ThE ChAsE

"This boy in my school was the cutest thing God could ever give females. He always wore these long braids in his hair and I was dying to touch them, but I knew I'd never be able to. So one day, I followed him around sneakily, holding a pair of scissors behind my back. I thought if I could get close enough I might be able to snip off a braid without him knowing and keep it for myself. It didn't work, though—he walked so fast! We never got together, but I was really obsessed with him."

On The Air

"I had a crush on this guy for the longest time. It was eating me up inside, so one day I told him to listen to his (and my) favorite radio station at 7:30 p.m. That night, I kept calling the station until the DJ picked up. At 7:30 (exactly), he answered and said, 'Hello, you're on the air, who do you want to give a shoutout to?' I said, 'Hey, this is Jennifer, and I want to tell Grant I like you—a lot!' I felt so much relief afterward, but I was nervous about what Grant thought of what I said.

Then ten minutes later, I heard Grant's voice on the radio. He said, 'Jennifer, I can't believe you like me. I like you too! See ya tomorrow at school. Meet me at the front entrance.' From then on, Grant and I were together—we still are!"

PuPPY LoVe

"I had just moved to a new neighborhood when I found out that one of the hottest guys in school lived five houses down from me. One day, when I was taking my dog for a walk, I spotted him on the street. I wanted to get his attention, so I 'accidentally' let go of my dog's leash. Luckily, she took off in his direction, forcing me to follow her. I ran over and struck up a conversation about hockey—turns out, we're both fans. He asked if I wanted to watch a game on TV the next day. My moment of canine bravery worked out, because we have been going out for over a year!"

red-letter day

"My guy once brought home these two big L-shaped bricks he found at work and gave them to me. He said he saw them, thought of me (my name is Lacy), and just knew I would like them. They still sit on my dresser to this day, but I have to admit, it's kind of weird!"

MaDe To OrDeR

"I had a huge crush on this hot guy who worked at a local restaurant. One day, I begged my friend to go there with me so that I could see him, but he wasn't there. So I wrote a little note on one of the restaurant's suggestion cards that said 'Your employees should start earlier (and Oscar should ask Fernanda out).' I put the card in the suggestion box, and then we left. About two days later, I saw Oscar at a party. Suddenly, he just came up to me and kissed me—and we've been dating ever since!"

ChErRy-Oh!

"I was out with a group of friends, including my crush. We ordered ice cream sundaes, but when they came out, my crush looked sad. I asked him what was wrong, and he said that he loved cherries—but this place didn't have them. So I excused myself, ran to the grocery store across the street, and bought a jar of cherries. I came back and put the jar next to his sundae, and when he saw them, he was so pumped that he asked me out on a date—for sundaes!"

ChIcKen Of ThE SwAmP

"I'm a pretty daring girl, but I have my limits and I usually never push them. Once when my family was on a cruise, I started hanging out with this guy I liked. On one of the islands we stopped at, they had alligator nuggets, which are like chicken nuggets made out of alligator meat. He dared me to try it. I was disgusted by the idea, but I really liked this guy so I agreed. He bought one and I dipped it in barbecue sauce. Surprisingly, it tasted like chicken! That night he told me how cool I was for trying the nugget, and then we hooked up!"

HoT CaKe

"I was at a birthday party and this hot guy had smeared cake all over himself. It was on his face, arms, clothes, pants, even around his mouth and on his palms. He went around asking everyone, 'Who will give me a hug?' No one dared to go near him. In fact, even the girls who thought he was hot all ran away, screaming, 'Eww! Stay away from me!' But I didn't. I went up to him and said, 'Okay, I'll hug you.' Ever since then, we've been dating."

TuBe-Y Or NoT TuBe-Y

"My friend had planned a houseboat trip and invited a few girls
and a few guys. When we got
there, we rode her uncle's ski
boat. All of the guys went out tub-
ing while all of the girls watched.
I wanted to impress my crush by
being the only girl to tube, so I
jumped in. Her uncle started
going as fast as he'd been pulling
the guys, and all of them were
cheering, even my crush. It felt so
awesome! Then he pushed it to
full throttle, and I hit this huge
wave and caught about 8 feet of

air, higher than any of the guys had gone. I landed it! When I got to the boat, my crush helped me out of the water and gave me a high-five. Later that night he took me to the top of the houseboat and we told each other how much we both liked one another. It was so cool!"

T-FlIrT

"I had a crush on this kid Timmy who was in my karate class. We liked the same bands, and I was determined to get him to like me through some crazy rock 'n' roll scheme. I decided to make a different shirt for every day—they would say 'My Heart Belongs To' someone from one of our favorite bands. I used Jim Morrison, Robert Plant, and about five more star names. Then, on the last day of class, I wrote 'My Heart Belongs to Timmy.' When he saw it, he asked me out!"

undercover brother

"This total cutie and his little brother always came into the store where I work. He never said a word—he just smiled, bought a few things, and left. I, of course, didn't say anything either because I was so hypnotized. He kept coming back, but we both wouldn't say anything. Then one day, his little brother came in alone, handed me a piece of paper, and walked out. I unfolded the paper, and it said 'Will you go out with my brother? He loses his voice when you're around!' "

GeTtIn' JiGgY WiTh It

"I was in the school library, and this guy I liked was there too. We started talking, and he dared me to do a jig. I wanted to impress him, so I accepted the dare and did an Irish jig in the middle of the crowded library! Everyone pointed, stared, and laughed—including my crush. Then the librarians threatened to kick me out for disrupting people. It was so embarrassing, and the guy thought I was insane for actually doing a jig in the library! We barely even speak now, but the whole thing was really funny."

SeRiOuS ChEmIsTrY

"Once in chemistry class, I was bragging about how good I was with chemicals. My crush over-heard me, so he came over to watch my experiment. I was about to add vinegar to the vial and he leaned over to see the liquids in the glass. I added the vinegar, and the concoction blew up in both of our faces! He gave me a 'What the heck was that about?' look, and then we just laughed. We've been dating ever since!"

CeLl MaTeS

"I have the same kind of cell phone as my crush. One day after school, we were waiting for the bus and I dropped my phone, so he picked it up. He had my phone in one hand and his in the other, and I accidentally took the wrong one. Later, my friend asked me why I hadn't replied to her text messages. I panicked and asked her what she had sent. She said, 'I asked if you were still in love with the sexy football player'—who happened to have my phone! The next day, he gave me my phone back and asked me out, saying, 'I didn't know you liked me. I like you too.' Now we're going out!"

love **BITES!**

"One night I called my boyfriend on his cell to tell him that I was on my way to his house to pick him up. He was on his way home and I got there first, so his mom invited me in to call him and let him know I was waiting. His friend answered and said he had bad news— my boyfriend wanted to dump me. Then his friend hung up. His mom asked me what happened, so I told her everything. She called them back and told them to come straight home and apologize to me. Now my friends and I laugh about what a turd he was for making his friend dump me so he wouldn't have to 'hear me cry.' Whenever I see him, I smile and think of how stupid he must've felt when his mom yelled at him in front of me!"

RoCkY MoUnTaIn HiGh

"I was giving ski lessons at a local resort, and I had a crush on this guy who was also a ski instructor. So just to impress him, I took red spray paint and wrote 'Erin loves Jack' in the snow on the side of the mountain. Then, when my crush was on his way up on the chair lift, he saw it and screamed out, 'I love you too, Erin!' It was absolutely incredible!"

GyM DaNdY

"I met this guy through some mutual friends. We hit it off but never hung out after that one time. Then one day I ran into him at the health club I go to. I started spending hours there, hoping I would run into him. We finally hung out again, but the relationship fizzled because it turned out that we didn't have a lot in common. No biggie—after all that time at the gym, I'm in the best shape I've ever been in my life!"

flower power

"It was Valentine's Day, and my boyfriend was going to make me dinner to celebrate. When I arrived at his house that night, dinner was on the table and there were tons of beautiful flowers, and he sweetly told me they were all there for me. Then I went to get something in the fridge, and there was a freakin' flower shop in there! When I asked him what the deal was, he admitted that he couldn't decide which flowers would be the best for me—so he bought them all!"

LoVe NoTeS

"It was my anniversary with my boyfriend and 'Back at One' by Brian McKnight had always been 'our song.' So I learned to play it on the piano. I was nervous because I don't like playing the piano in front of people, but I did great. He said it was one of the sweetest things I'd ever done for him! There was definitely no singing involved though."

BlInD AmBiTiOn

"I liked my friend Josh, but he was always chasing other girls. So I sent him an AOL InstaKiss from his 'secret admirer' and left a note in his locker that said 'Meet me at the park blindfold-ed.' Later, he was sitting on this bench, and I took off the blind-fold. He was amazed at my seize-the-day attitude—we just had our six-month anniversary!"